Fanciful Faces & Handbound Books
FAIRY TALES

Fanciful Faces & Handbound Books
FAIRY TALES

by Ron and Marsha Feller

designed and illustrated by Kathryn Kusché Hastings

ΑℲF The Arts Factory, Seattle, Washington

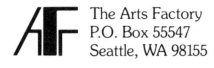

The Arts Factory
P.O. Box 55547
Seattle, WA 98155

Library of Congress Cataloging in
Publication Data

Feller, Ron, 1942-
   Fairy tales.

   (Fanciful faces & handbound books)
   Bibliography: p.
   Summary: Instructions for making paper masks of
fairy tale characters and making a fairy tale book
through the process of writing and illustrating a story
and binding it into a French-fold book.
   1. Books—Juvenile literature.   2. Masks—Juvenile literature.
3. Book design—Juvenile literature.   4. Creative writing—Juvenile
literature.   5. Fairy tales—Authorship—Juvenile literature.
[1. Books. 2. Masks. 3. Handicraft.   4. Creative writing.
5. Fairy tales—Authorship]   I. Feller, Marsha, 1944-   .
II. Hastings, Kathryn Kusché, ill.   III. Title.
IV. Series: Feller, Ron, 1942-
Fanciful faces & handbound books.
Z4.Z9F43   1989   808′.066398   88-34952
ISBN 0-9615873-1-8

Editor: Phyllis Luvera Ennes
Photographer: Andrew P. Smith

To Dort, with love

How to get into this book—

Knock at the knocker on the door,
Pull the bell at the side,
Then, if you are very quiet,
You will hear a teeny tiny voice
Say through the grating,
"Take down the key . . ."
Put the key in the keyhole,
Which it fits exactly,
Unlock the door, and
WALK IN.

— *Joseph Jacobs*

How to Use This Book

This book is about a process—a writing process that can help you become a published young author. You simply do the entire procedure yourself. You write, illustrate, make the page layout, print, and bind the pages. You have just published a book.

Of course, you need inspiration for writing, and there are many ways to find that inspiration. One way is to create a mask character first; then write about it. Use the character as a springboard for your writing. This book will show you how to make masks of a king, a queen, a dragon, and a wizard. It will even show you how to make a mask of yourself. (After all, your story may need a hero or heroine much like you.) Then it will show you how to write your very own story in the style of a fairy tale.

To get started, make one or several of the mask characters, and write your fairy tale. Then lay out the pages, draw the illustrations, and write or type out the story. After that, bind the pages, decorate the cover . . . and you have a real book. You are a published author.

When you have finished this process, you will have a unique handbound book of which you can be proud, plus a mask of the character that inspired your writing. Later, you can make a mask display on your wall, or turn your story into a play and use the masks to dramatize the story.

After you make one book, chances are you will want to make more. Try the process again. Create different characters and write a different fairy tale. As you make more and more books, you will discover how much fun it is to become a "published" young author. So get ready to take the first step. . . .

DON'T HESITATE . . . PARTICIPATE!

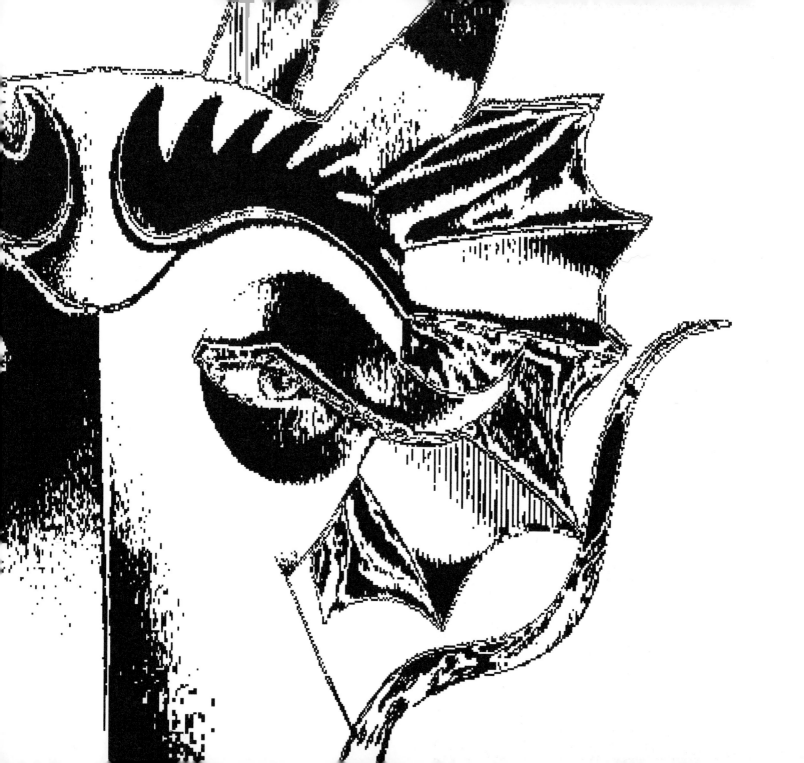

MASKS

Choose one of the following masks. Follow the step-by-step directions to create a wonderful character that can inspire you when you write your fairy tale.

Materials for Making the Masks

Basic materials (shown left):
Construction paper, 12"x 18", 9"x 12", 6"x 9"
Elmer's Glue-All
Pencil
Scissors
Cardboard rod from a clothes hanger
Masking tape

Optional (shown right):
X-acto knife
Self-healing cutting mat
Ribbon shredder (see page 21 for directions)
Curling ribbon
3D-Os (small adhesive backed foam cylinders for adding dimension)
Foam rubber
Oil pastels
Cotton balls

Specialty papers
(left to right)
Alligator Skin
Foil Paper
Strathmore 300
   Colored Art Paper
Velour Paper
Moonscape

KING

You can make the king in the photograph, or you can change the shapes and decorations to make your own version of the king.

1. Basic Shape

Fold a sheet of 12" x 18" construction paper in half lengthwise. Draw half of an oval from the fold. Cut out the shape.

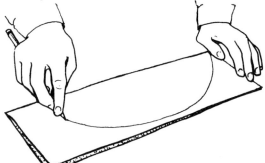

2. Hair, Sideburns, and Beard

Fold a sheet of 12" x 18" construction paper in half lengthwise. Place the folded head shape along the folded paper, matching the folds. Trace a dotted guideline around the edge of the face shape.

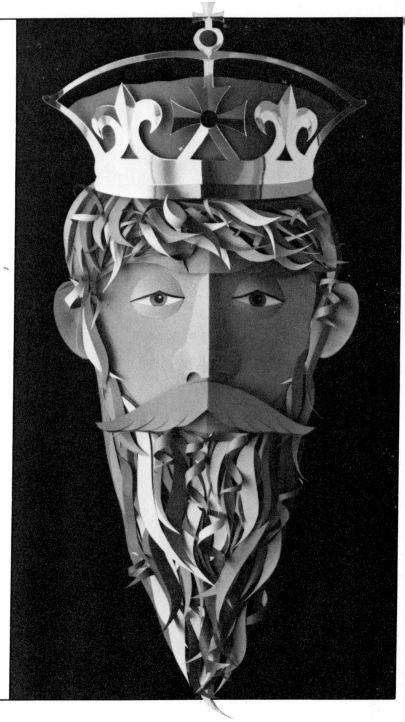

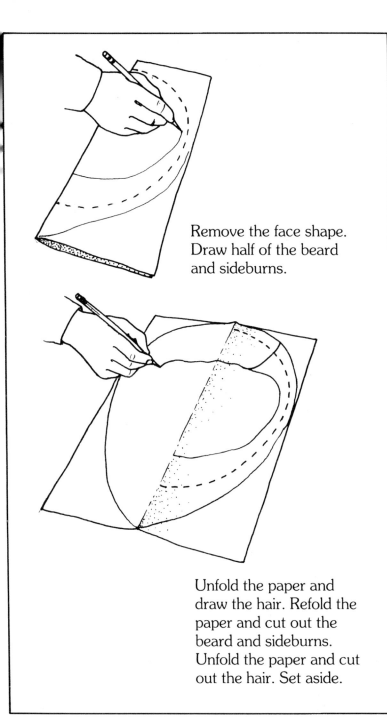

Remove the face shape. Draw half of the beard and sideburns.

Unfold the paper and draw the hair. Refold the paper and cut out the beard and sideburns. Unfold the paper and cut out the hair. Set aside.

3. Nose

Fold a rectangular sheet of 6"x9" paper in half lengthwise. Cut one half of the nose shape from the fold. Draw it first, if necessary. (Reverse the fold to hide any pencil lines.)

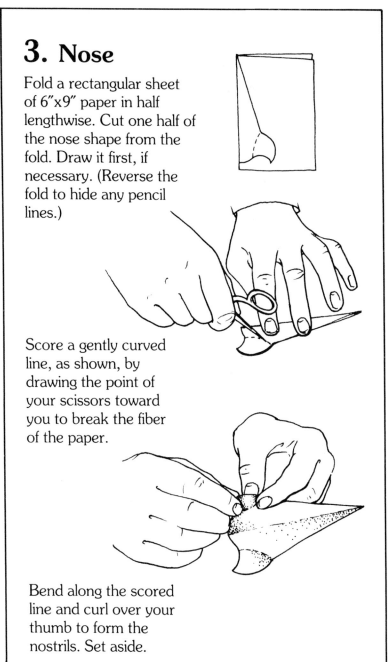

Score a gently curved line, as shown, by drawing the point of your scissors toward you to break the fiber of the paper.

Bend along the scored line and curl over your thumb to form the nostrils. Set aside.

4. Forehead and Brow

Fold a sheet of 9"x12" paper in half widthwise and place under the top part of the face shape. Trace around the top part of the face shape.

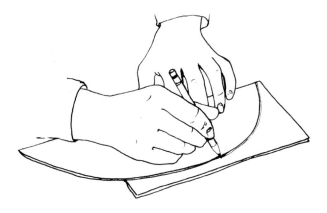

Lift the face shape and draw the brow line. Cut out the forehead and the brow.

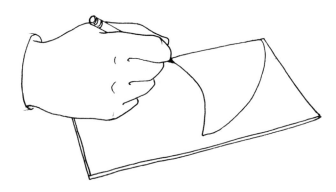

5. Gluing the Nose and Brow

Position the nose and the brow on the face. Crease the bridge of the nose well. Run a bead of glue along the edges of the nose, as shown. (Be careful not to flatten the nose when attaching.)

Run a bead of glue around the upper curved edge of the brow. Glue in place. (The middle part of the brow should overlap the nose slightly.)

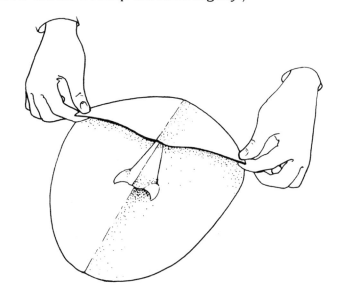

6. Eyes

Use three different colors of construction paper to make the parts of the eyes (eyeball, iris, pupil). Make the eyeball first. Remember, if you cut one eyeball from two pieces or from a folded sheet of paper, you will have two the same shape. Cut out and add the irises and pupils of each eye.

Make the eyes "come to life" by adding a highlight spot to each pupil. Fold a scrap of light paper and cut a tiny piece. Glue in place. Glue the eyes to the mask.

7. Eyelids

Fold a scrap of paper and cut the upper eyelid shape. Fold another scrap of paper, and cut the lower eyelid shape slightly smaller than the upper eyelid.

Make the dark accent line on the upper lids. Fold a scrap of dark paper. Place the eyelid on the dark paper and trace around the bottom of the eyelid shape. Remove the eyelid and draw another line slightly above the first line. Cut out the accent line and glue along the edge of the eyelid.

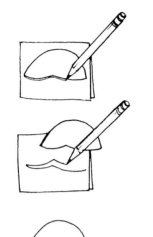

Curve the eyelids between your thumb and index finger.

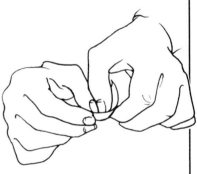

Run a bead of glue along the outside edge of the eyelids and set one above and one below the eyes so the lids meet at the corners. (Don't push too hard . . . let the glue do the work.)

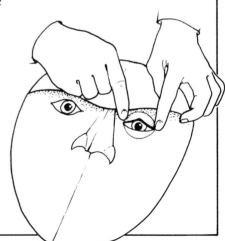

8. Mouth

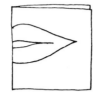

Fold a scrap of paper and cut out half the mouth from the fold. Cut a thin section in the center of the mouth, from the fold, to form the upper and lower lips. Glue mouth in place.

Note: The mouth does not have to be glued down flat. To give a raised effect to the lips, spot glue at the corners. Position the mouth so that it is slightly lifted from the basic head shape. Hold until glue sets.

9. Ears

Fold a piece of paper in half and cut a rounded shape from the outside edge of the paper. Add dimension to the ears by cutting a slit at the base of each ear, overlapping, and gluing.

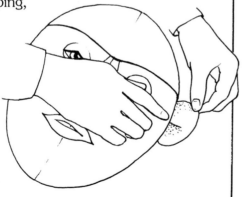

Run a bead of glue along the base of the inside of the ears and attach to the sides of the face shape from the back side of the mask.

10. Gluing Hair, Sideburns, and Beard

Reverse the fold of the hair, sideburns, and beard to hide any pencil lines. Position the hair, sideburns, and beard on the face. Run a bead of glue around the inside edge of the hair, sideburns, and beard piece. Glue in place.

11. Adding Dimension to the Hair, Sideburns, and Beard

Fold a sheet of 12"x18" paper into fourths. Starting from one side, cut out a soft "s" shape. Continue cutting these "s" shapes in a series. (The number of pieces will vary according to the size of the "s" shapes.) Cut as many pieces as needed to fill the hair, sideburns, and beard.

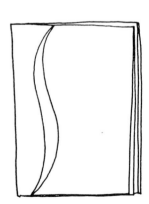

Curl or score the "s" shapes:

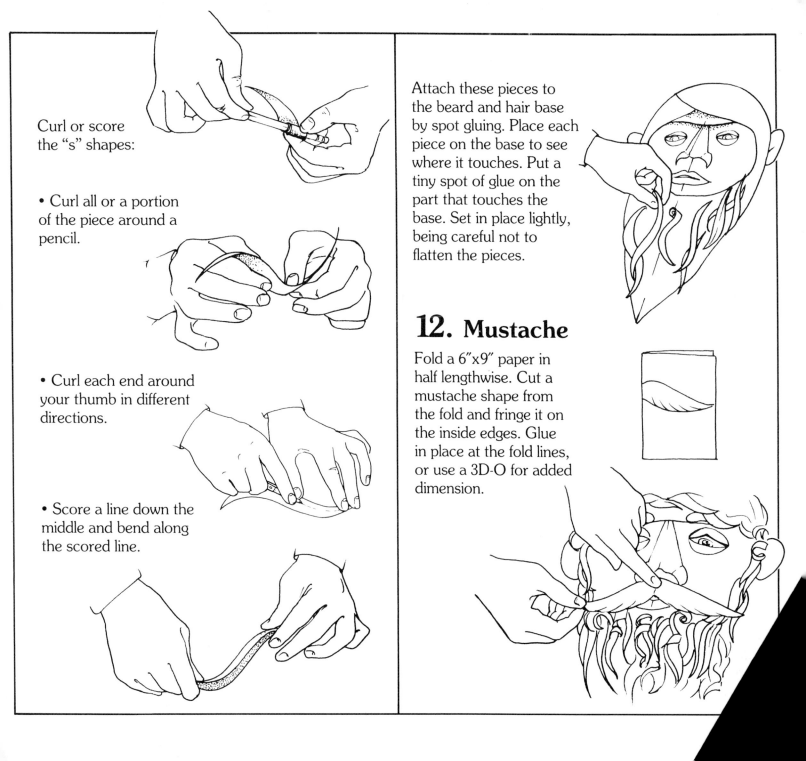

• Curl all or a portion of the piece around a pencil.

• Curl each end around your thumb in different directions.

• Score a line down the middle and bend along the scored line.

Attach these pieces to the beard and hair base by spot gluing. Place each piece on the base to see where it touches. Put a tiny spot of glue on the part that touches the base. Set in place lightly, being careful not to flatten the pieces.

12. Mustache

Fold a 6"x9" paper in half lengthwise. Cut a mustache shape from the fold and fringe it on the inside edges. Glue in place at the fold lines, or use a 3D-O for added dimension.

13. Eyebrows

Cut two identical eyebrows from a folded scrap of paper. Fringe the edges and glue to the brow.

14. Crown

Fold a sheet of 9"x12" paper in half widthwise. (Foil paper makes the crown look as if it's made of gold or silver.) Draw half of a crown from the fold. Cut out the crown shape using scissors or an X-acto knife and a cutting mat.

Note: If using foil paper, make a crown template from construction paper. Then trace around the template on the back of the foil paper and cut.

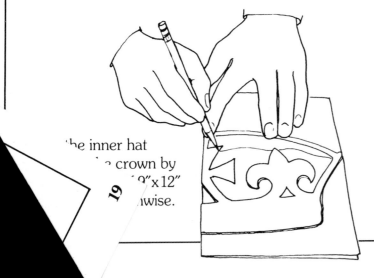

the inner hat
crown by
9"x12"
wise.

(Velour paper makes the inner hat look as if it's made of velvet.) Place the folded crown along the folded sheet of paper. Trace around the bottom and sides of the crown. Remove the crown and finish drawing the top of the inner hat piece. Cut out the inner hat piece and set aside.

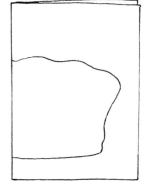

Place the crown face down. Score and fold the ornate sections for added dimension, if desired.

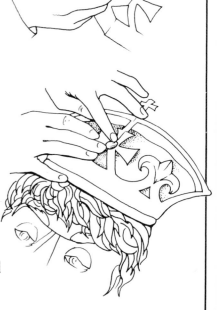

Turn the crown face up and decorate with paper "jewels" and other accents. (Foil paper, sequins, or old costume jewelry may be used for a dramatic effect.) Separate the crown and inner hat piece with 3D-Os, foam rubber, or folded paper springs to add dimension. Run a bead of glue along the bottom of the crown and set in place.

15. Color Accent

Rub oil pastels on a cotton ball and "dust" the cheeks, lips, nose, and ears for additional color, if desired.

16. Attaching a Rod

Make this a hand-held mask by attaching a clothes hanger rod, a 12″ stick, or a 12″ x 18″ sheet of tightly rolled paper to the back of the mask with masking tape.

17. Adding Ribbon

Add shredded ribbon or fabric ribbon to the rod for a festive decoration, if desired.

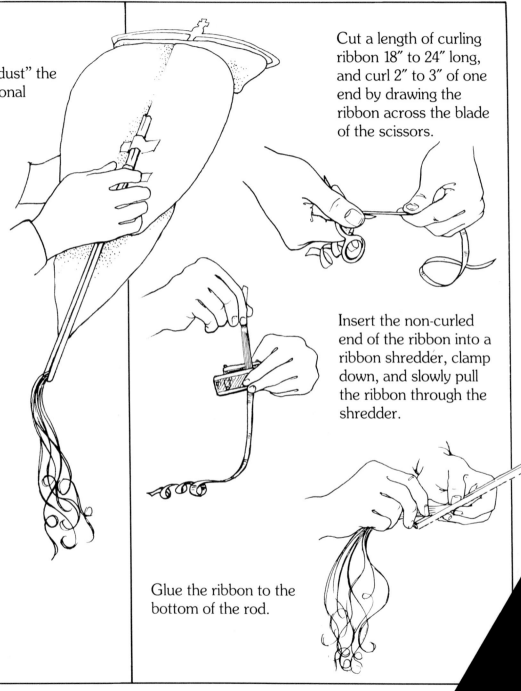

Cut a length of curling ribbon 18″ to 24″ long, and curl 2″ to 3″ of one end by drawing the ribbon across the blade of the scissors.

Insert the non-curled end of the ribbon into a ribbon shredder, clamp down, and slowly pull the ribbon through the shredder.

Glue the ribbon to the bottom of the rod.

QUEEN

You can make the queen in the photograph, or you can change the shapes and decorations to make your own version of the queen.

1. Basic Shape

Fold a sheet of 12″x18″ construction paper in half lengthwise. Draw half of an oval from the fold. Cut out the shape.

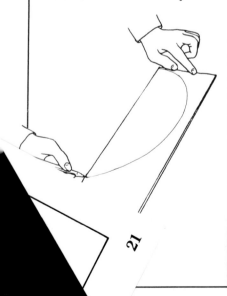

2. Hair

Fold two sheets (two different colors) of 12"x18" construction paper in half widthwise. Place one sheet inside the other.

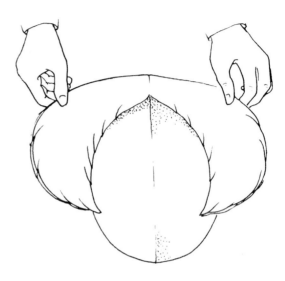

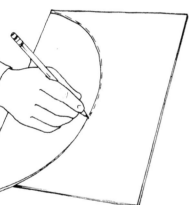

Place the folded head shape along the folded paper, matching the folds. Trace a dotted guideline around the edge of the face shape. Remove the face shape.

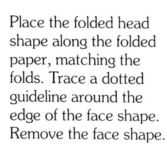

Draw the outside and the inside of the hair. Cut out the hair. Fringe the outside and the inside of the hair.

Unfold the hair shapes and glue together along the folds. Glue the hair in place.

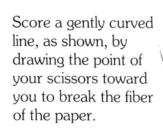

3. Nose

Fold a rectangular sheet of 6"x9" paper in half lengthwise. Cut half of the nose shape from the fold. Draw it first, if necessary.

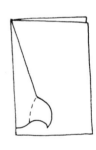

Score a gently curved line, as shown, by drawing the point of your scissors toward you to break the fiber of the paper.

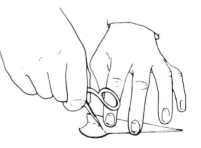

Bend along the scored line and curl over your thumb to form the nostrils. Glue the nose in place.

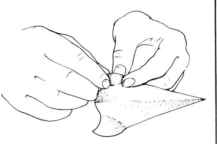

4. Eyes

Use three different colors of construction paper to make the parts of the eyes (eyeball, iris, pupil). Make the eyeball first. Remember, if you cut one eyeball from two pieces or from a folded sheet of paper, you will have two the same shape.

Cut out and add the irises and pupils of each eye. Make the eyes "come to life" by adding a highlight spot to each pupil. Fold a scrap of light-colored paper and cut a tiny piece. Glue in place. Glue the eyes to the mask.

5. Eyelids

Fold a scrap of paper and cut the upper eyelid shape.

Fold a scrap of paper and cut the lower eyelid shape slightly narrower than the upper eyelid shape.

Make the dark accent line on the upper lids. Fold a scrap of dark paper. Place the eyelid on the dark paper and trace around the bottom of the eyelid shape.

Remove the eyelid and draw another line slightly above the first line.

Cut out the accent line and glue along the edge of the eyelid.

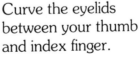

Curve the eyelids between your thumb and index finger.

Run a bead of glue along the outside edge of the eyelids and set above and below the eyes so the lids meet at the corners.

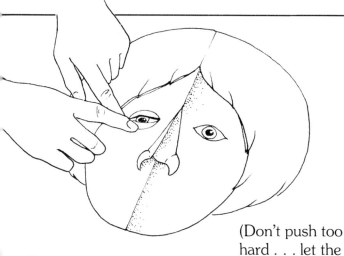

6. Eyebrows

Fold a scrap of paper and cut the eyebrow shape. Glue the eyebrows in place.

(Don't push too hard . . . let the glue do the work.)

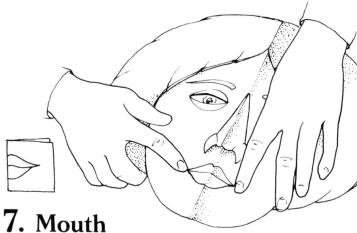

7. Mouth

Fold a scrap of paper and cut out half an upper lip and half a lower lip. Draw the lips first, if desired. Glue the lips in place.

8. Crown

Fold a sheet of 9" x 12" paper in half widthwise. (Foil paper makes the crown look as if it's made of gold or silver.) Draw half of a crown from the fold.

Cut out the crown shape using scissors or an X-acto knife and a cutting mat.

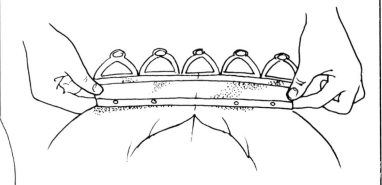

Decorate the crown as desired. Run a bead of glue along the bottom of the crown and set in place.

9. Color Accent

Rub oil pastels on a cotton ball and "dust" the cheeks, lips, nose, and ears for additional color, if desired.

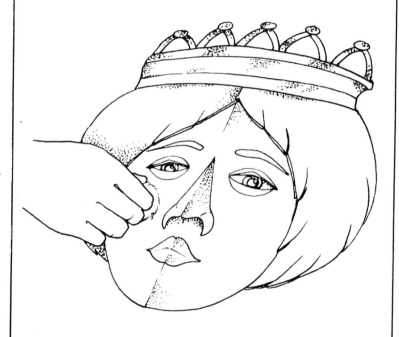

10. Attaching a Rod

Make this a hand-held mask by attaching a clothes hanger rod, a 12" stick, or a piece of tightly rolled paper to the back of the mask with masking tape.

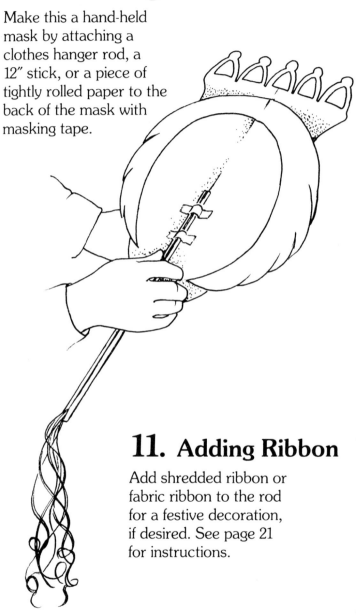

11. Adding Ribbon

Add shredded ribbon or fabric ribbon to the rod for a festive decoration, if desired. See page 21 for instructions.

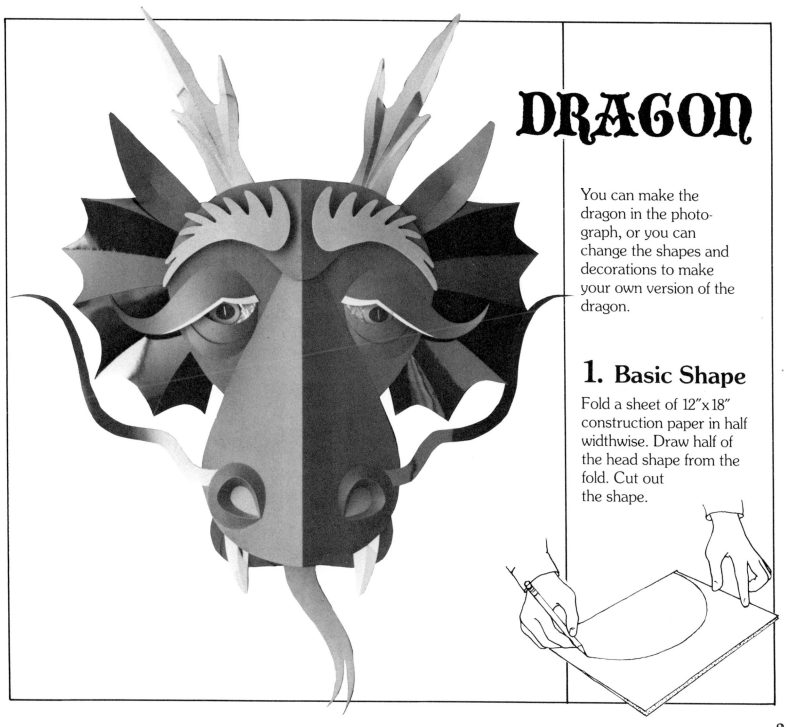

DRAGON

You can make the dragon in the photograph, or you can change the shapes and decorations to make your own version of the dragon.

1. Basic Shape

Fold a sheet of 12″ x 18″ construction paper in half widthwise. Draw half of the head shape from the fold. Cut out the shape.

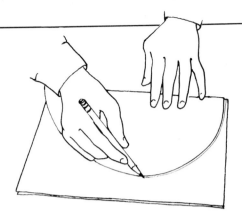

2. Forehead and Brow

Fold a sheet of 12"x 18" construction paper in half widthwise and place under the top part of the face shape. Trace around the top part of the face shape.

Lift the face shape and draw the brow line. Cut out the forehead and brow. Set aside.

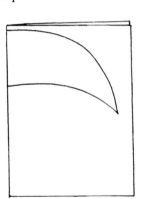

3. Snout

Fold a sheet of 12"x 18" construction paper in half lengthwise. Draw half of the snout from the fold. Cut out the shape.

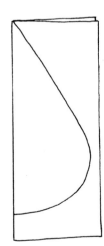

4. Gluing the Snout and Brow

Position the snout and brow on the face.

Run a bead of glue along the edges of the snout and attach in a raised position.

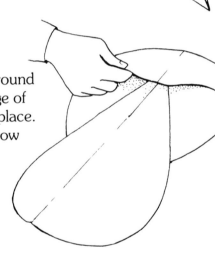

Run a bead of glue around the upper curved edge of the brow and glue in place. (The middle of the brow should overlap the snout slightly.)

5. Lower Jaw

Fold a sheet of 6"x9" paper in half widthwise. Draw half of the lower jaw from the fold. Cut out the shape. Fringe the lower jaw.

Run a bead of glue along the upper third of the mountain fold, turn the lower jaw over, and glue in place under the snout. This creates the open mouth of the dragon.

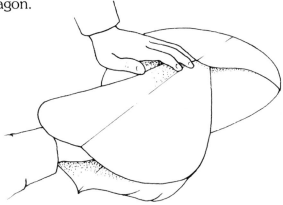

6. Fangs

Fold a scrap of paper and cut out a long tooth shape. Score a line down the center of each fang by drawing the point of your scissors toward you to break the fiber of the paper. Bend along the scored lines to give the fangs dimension. Spot glue the fangs into position.

7. Tongue

Draw a snake-like tongue on a scrap of paper. Cut out the tongue; shape by curling over your thumb.

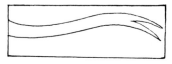

Glue in place.

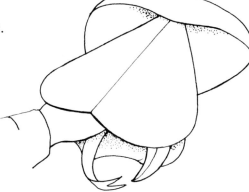

8. Nostrils

Fold a sheet of 6"x9" paper in half widthwise. Draw a crescent shape, as shown. Cut out the shape.

Score a line down the center of each crescent shape. Bend along the scored line and glue at the tips.

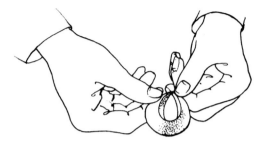

Glue a background color, cut from scraps, behind the nostrils, if desired. Run a bead of glue along the outside edge of the nostrils and set in place.

9. Eyes

Use three different colors of paper to make the eyes (eyeball, iris, pupil). Make the eyeball first, then cut out the iris and pupil. (Remember to fold each color of paper before cutting in order to make two pieces the same shape.) Plastic papers such as Moonscape or Alligator Skin will give the eyes a fiery appearance. Fold a scrap of light-colored paper and cut a thin, narrow piece. Glue to the pupils to add a highlight to the eyes. Glue the eyes to the mask.

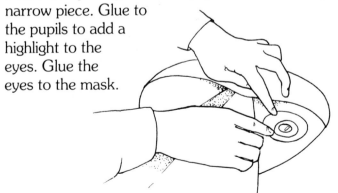

10. Eyelids

Fold a sheet of 6"x9" paper twice and cut the lower eyelid shapes. (This makes four eyelid shapes—two lower lids for each eye.)

Curve the lower lids between your thumb and index finger.

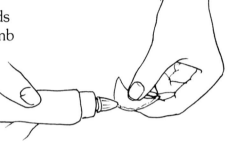

Run a bead of glue along the outside edge of the eyelids and glue in place below the eyes.

Fold a sheet of 6"x9" paper and cut the upper eyelid shapes.

Make the accent line on the upper lids. Fold a scrap of dark paper. Place the eyelid on the paper and trace around the bottom of the eyelid shape.

Remove the eyelid and draw another line slightly above the first line.

Cut out the accent line and glue along the edge of the eyelid.

Curve the eyelids between your thumb and index finger. Run a bead of glue along the outside edge of the eyelids and set in place above the eyes.

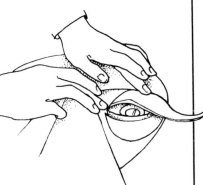

11. Eyebrows

Fold a sheet of 9″ x 12″ paper in half widthwise. Draw the eyebrow shape. Cut out and glue in place or use 3D-Os, foam rubber, or paper springs for added dimension.

12. Ears

Fold a sheet of 9″ x 12″ paper in half widthwise. Draw an ear and cut out the shape.

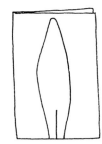

Add dimension to the ears by cutting a slit at the base of each ear.

Overlap and glue the tabs. Run a bead of glue along the base of the inside of the ear and attach to the head from the back side of the mask.

13. Horns

Fold a sheet of 9″ x 12″ paper in half lengthwise. Draw a horn shape and cut from the outside edge of the paper. Score and bend, as shown. Glue into place behind the head.

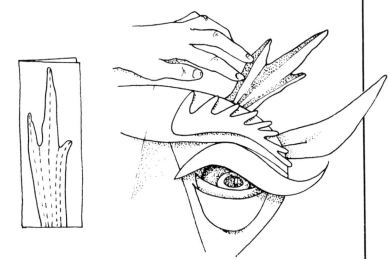

14. Neck Frill

Fold a sheet of 12″ x 18″ paper in half widthwise. Draw the neck frill and score as shown.

Cut out the neck frill shape. Fold the scored lines in an accordion fashion to indicate the spines of the neck frill. Glue in place at either side of the head from the back side of the mask.

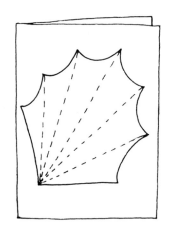

15. Feelers

Fold a sheet of 12″ x 18″ construction paper lengthwise. Draw a snake-like shape, pointed at one end. Cut out and glue to the side of each nostril.

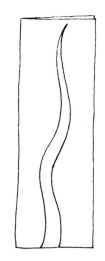

16. Attaching a Rod

Make this a hand-held mask by attaching a clothes hanger rod, a 12″ stick, or a piece of tightly rolled paper to the back of the mask with masking tape.

17. Adding Ribbon

Add shredded ribbon or fabric ribbon to the rod for a festive decoration, if desired.
See page 21 for instructions.

WIZARD

You can make the wizard in the photograph, or you can change the shapes and decorations to make your own version of the wizard.

The wizard is similar to the king. There are only a few changes—the crown and the hat are the most obvious.

Make the wizard by following the directions for most of the features of the king. The order in which you make and glue the features is slightly different, however.

Use the following order to make the wizard. Check the instructions in the king section. Follow the specific directions in this section for the beard and sideburns, and for the hat.

1. Basic Shape

See page 14.

2. Nose

See page 15.

3. Forehead and Brow

See page 16.

4. Gluing Nose and Brow

See page 16.

5. Eyes

See page 17.

6. Eyelids

See page 17.

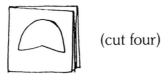

(cut four)

7. Mouth

See page 18.

8. Ears

See page 18.

9. Beard and Sideburns

Fold a sheet of 12″ x 18″ construction paper in half lengthwise. Place the center of the mask along the folded edge of the paper. Draw a dotted guideline around the edge of the mask.

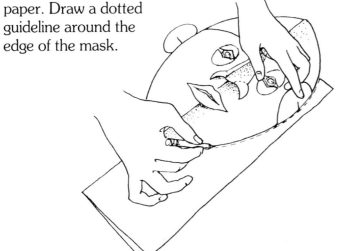

Remove the mask, and draw half of the beard and sideburns. Cut out the beard and sideburns and fringe. Reverse the fold of the beard and sideburns in order to hide the guideline.

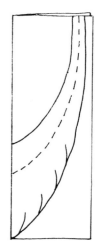

Run a bead of glue along the inside edge of the beard and sideburns, and glue in place.

10. Adding Dimension to the Beard See pages 18 and 19.

11. Mustache

See page 19.

12. Eyebrows

See page 20.

13. Hat

Place the mask on the lower section of a sheet of *unfolded* 12"x18" paper. (Velour paper makes the hat look as if it's made of velvet.) Mark the paper where the bottom of the hat will fit over the forehead.

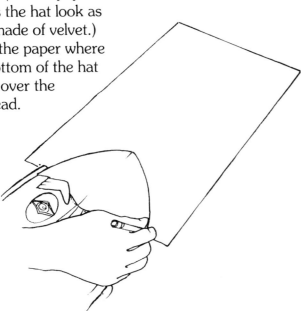

Remove the mask, and draw the hat shape.

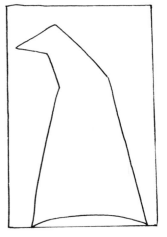

Cut out the hat and decorate with quarter moons and stars. (Silver foil paper, aluminum foil, or silver contact paper may be used for a more dazzling effect.)

Run a bead of glue along the bottom edge of the hat and set in place.

14. Color Accent

See page 21.

15. Attaching a Rod

See page 21.

16. Adding a Ribbon

See page 21.

HERO & HEROINE

After you have made one or more of the fanciful fairy tale masks, you may want to make a mask of yourself because the hero or heroine of a fairy tale is often a young person. If you do, you may also want to disguise yourself by changing your appearance slightly, or by adding a hat, crown, or helmet.

Answer these questions before you begin:

• Will you be a prince or a princess? an apprentice or a servant? an ordinary villager or a knight?

• Will you have long hair or short hair? freckles or rosy cheeks? a big smile or none?

Now look in the mirror and take a mental picture of yourself. Make a quick sketch of your face as you would like it to look in mask form.

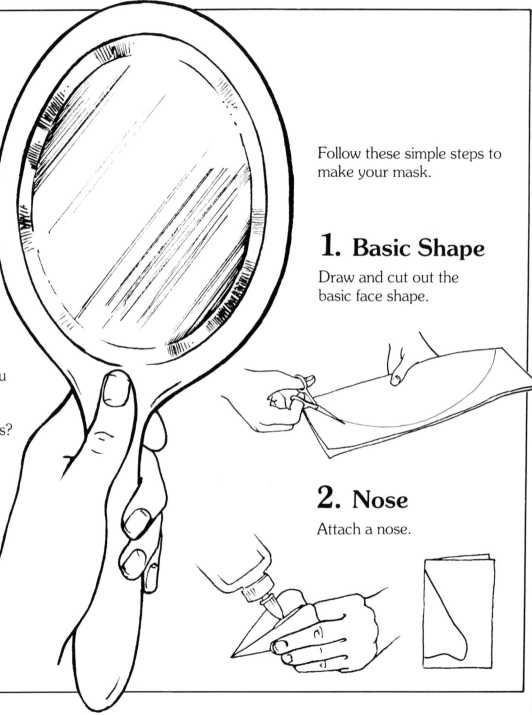

Follow these simple steps to make your mask.

1. Basic Shape

Draw and cut out the basic face shape.

2. Nose

Attach a nose.

3. Eyes

Cut out the eyeballs, irises, pupils, and highlights. Glue to the mask.

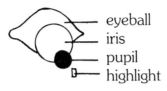

eyeball
iris
pupil
highlight

4. Eyelids

Cut the eyelids. Curve by drawing over your thumb, and glue in place.

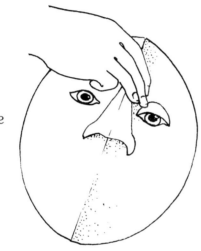

Note: If eyelashes are desired, add them before gluing the eyelids in place.

5. Eyebrows

Cut the eyebrows and glue above the eyes.

6. Ears

Glue the ears behind the back sides of the mask.

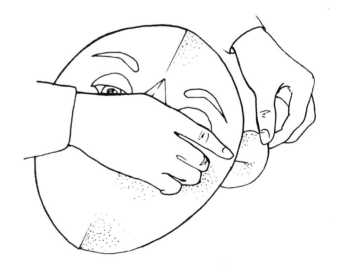

7. Mouth

Attach the mouth.

8. Hair

Cut out the hair and glue to the mask.

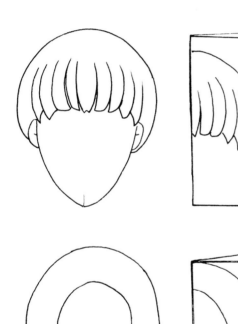

9. Crown, Hat, or Helmet

Add a crown, hat, or helmet if desired.

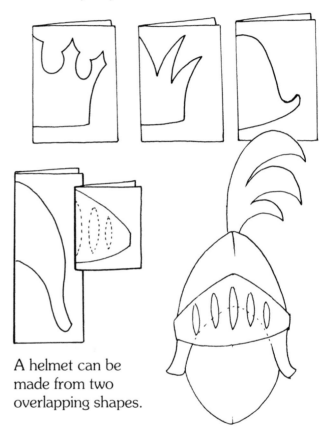

A helmet can be made from two overlapping shapes.

10. Rod

Attach a rod to the back of the mask. See page 21.

11. Ribbon

Add ribbon. See page 21 for directions.

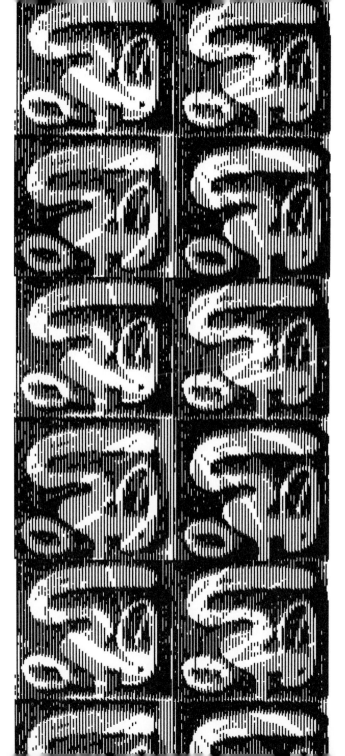

FAIRY TALES

Now that you have created your mask character or characters, you are ready to begin writing your fairy tale. After it is written, you will want to illustrate your story. It's a good idea to visualize the pictures in your mind as you are writing. The following pages will give you some good tips for writing and illustrating your fairy tale.

Tips for Writing Fairy Tales

Fairy tales are stories that have been passed by word of mouth from adults to children for hundreds of years. These stories have become part of the folklore of the people. Every time the stories were told they changed slightly because every storyteller told them in his or her own way. Finally, in the late 1600s, people began to write down these stories and print them in books. Charles Perrault, Joseph Jacobs, and Jacob and Wilhelm Grimm collected and published many fairy tales.

People of all ages enjoyed these tales, and some people even began to write stories in the same style. Hans Christian Andersen is probably the most famous author of stories written in the style of fairy tales.

You can do the same thing. Just keep these basic tips in mind when you write your own story in a fairy tale style.

- **The story takes place long ago and far away.**
  No definite place or time is stated. Fairy tales often begin like this: "Long ago in a land far away from here . . ." or "Once upon a time in a distant land . . ."

- **Magical things can happen in the story— things that could never happen in the real world.**
  Animals can talk, horses can fly, and frogs can turn into princes.

- **There are magical characters in the story.**
  There are giants, wizards, dragons, witches, dwarfs, trolls, fairies, ogres, and talking animals in fairy tales.

- **Problems must be solved by either a person or a family.**
  Jack in "Jack and the Beanstalk" and a family of pigs in "The Three Little Pigs" are examples.

- **Young people are often the heroes or heroines.**
  They are often orphans, abandoned, or the youngest members of their families, but they are ordinary people like you or me.

- **Characters are one-dimensional.**
  They are either good or bad, hardworking or lazy, smart or stupid, beautiful or ugly.

- **Characters are never given names as we know them.**
  Characters are not given names like Susan, David, or Timmy; instead, they are either not named (the boy, the giant, the princess, or the fairy godmother) or they are given names that describe the character in some way (Little Red Riding Hood, Beauty, Tom Thumb, or Cinderella). "Jack" and "Hansel and Gretel" are really generic names; that is, "Jack" stands for "a boy," and "Hansel and Gretel" stand for "a brother and a sister."

- **Good always wins over evil.**
  Jack outwits the giant; the wicked witch in "Snow White and the Seven Dwarfs" is foiled; and the third little pig outsmarts the big, bad wolf.

- **The plot is simple.**
  It is basically a series of events. The hero or heroine must solve a problem. He or she must struggle against many obstacles. The hero or heroine overcomes the trials and is triumphant.

- **The hero or heroine is often helped along the way.**
  Birds and animals, things from nature (such as trees), other people, or magical characters offer help and guide the hero or heroine along the way when it is necessary.

- **Virtues help the hero or heroine overcome obstacles.**
  The hero or heroine may possess one or more of the following virtues: kindness, courage, thoughtfulness, honor, patience, truthfulness, ability to take advice, ability to think quickly, humility.

- **The story has a happy ending.**
  A fairy tale gives the listener or reader hope for the future—that no matter how difficult things seem to be, the hero or heroine will be rewarded in the end, and will live "happily ever after."

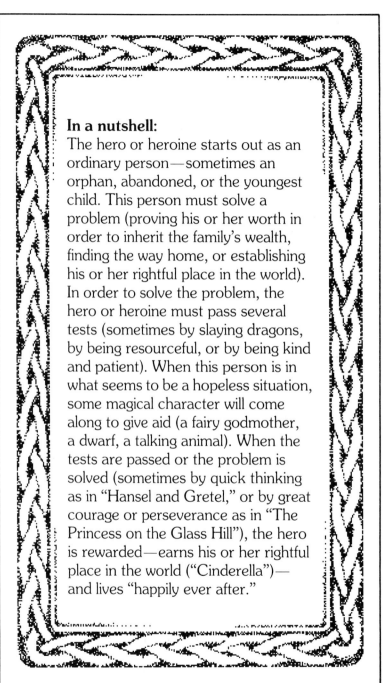

In a nutshell:
The hero or heroine starts out as an ordinary person—sometimes an orphan, abandoned, or the youngest child. This person must solve a problem (proving his or her worth in order to inherit the family's wealth, finding the way home, or establishing his or her rightful place in the world). In order to solve the problem, the hero or heroine must pass several tests (sometimes by slaying dragons, by being resourceful, or by being kind and patient). When this person is in what seems to be a hopeless situation, some magical character will come along to give aid (a fairy godmother, a dwarf, a talking animal). When the tests are passed or the problem is solved (sometimes by quick thinking as in "Hansel and Gretel," or by great courage or perseverance as in "The Princess on the Glass Hill"), the hero is rewarded—earns his or her rightful place in the world ("Cinderella")— and lives "happily ever after."

To begin writing your fairy tale, ask yourself these questions:

What will the **setting** be? Describe it—paint a picture with words.

What **characters** will be in the story? Who will be the hero or heroine? Who will be the magical characters?

What will be the main **problem** to solve?

How will the hero or heroine find a **solution**? What obstacles will be placed in the hero's or heroine's path?

What will be the **reward**?

Now, open up your mind, let your imagination play, and have fun writing your fairy tale.

Tips for Illustrating

Now that you've written your fairy tale, it's time to plan your illustrations. You may decide to have just a few illustrations, or you may decide to have an illustration on every page like some of the popular picture books.

Many illustrators have become well-known for their wonderful illustrations of fairy tales. Go to the library and look for fairy tales illustrated by some of these famous illustrators: Nancy Ekholm Burkert, Michael Hague, Trina Schart Hyman, Susan Jeffers, Mercer Mayer, Kay Nielsen, Margaret Evans Price, Howard Pyle, Arthur Rackham, Ruth Sanderson, Paul O. Zelinsky. This is one way to get inspiration for your own illustrations. Continue reading this section for more ideas.

• **Read your story two or three times.** Try to see the pictures in your mind as you read. This may help you decide on the number of illustrations you want and where you want them to appear in your story.

• **Use your "mind's eye" to see a picture in different ways.** Pretend you are looking at a scene through a camera.

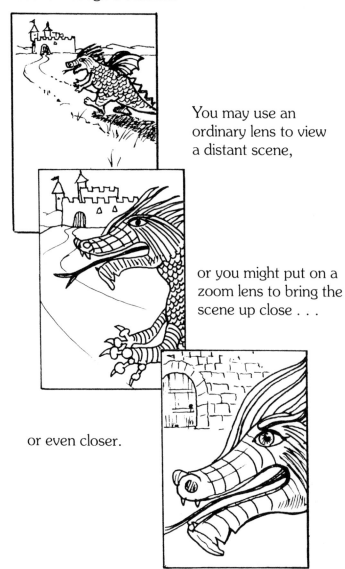

You may use an ordinary lens to view a distant scene,

or you might put on a zoom lens to bring the scene up close . . .

or even closer.

Experiment with
different ways of
showing the
same scene.

*"The wizard
suddenly appeared."*

• **Block out your drawing by using basic
shapes.** Does your subject have any of these
shapes?

- **Show perspective (depth and distance) by drawing the objects that appear close to you larger than the objects that appear farther from you.** Draw a background object around, not through, a foreground object. This **overlapping** technique also helps show perspective.

- **Make something look very large by making everything around it very small.**

- **Draw the main objects first, then add the details.**

- **Use your mask characters as models when you draw them.** Try to put the same details in your illustrations that you put in your mask.

- **Show different expressions by how you draw the eyes, eyebrows, and mouth.**

Round eyes, curved eyebrows, and up-turned mouth show friendliness.

Round eyes, raised eyebrows, and open mouth show surprise.

Drooping eyes, eyebrows, and mouth show sadness.

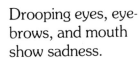

Narrow eyes, "v"-placed eyebrows, and straight mouth show anger.

- **Think about how you will place your text with your illustrations.** Will it be above, below, down one side, wrapped around? (You can use any or all of these arrangements.) The examples below will help you plan.

- **Make some quick, rough sketches on scratch paper.** Show the placement of the illustration and text for each page. Save these rough sketches until you are ready to make the final illustrations. The next section will tell you how to carry out your plans to make your book.

THE HANDBOUND BOOK

You've made your character or characters, written your fairy tale, and made some quick sketches of illustrations you want to include in your book. Now, all you need to do is lay out the pages, print them, and bind them into a book. One of the easiest ways to make a book is to print on only one side of the paper. After printing, the pages are folded in the center with writing on the outside, stacked, and bound on the open edge. This French-fold page will be used in the book you will make.

The French-fold book is bound on the open edge.

Materials for Making the Book

Paper: unruled, white, 8½"x11"
Pencil or black, fine line pen
Typewriter, if you type
Computer, if you use a word processor
Scissors or paper cutter
Glue stick or Mystic Tape
Heavy-duty stapler
Ruler
Bookbinding tape, 1½" wide
Use of a photocopy machine, if you want to make
    several copies of your book
Endpapers: construction paper
Cover board: poster board, railroad board, or any
    heavy weight board that has a plain surface
Guide form: for the page layout (See page 53 for
    directions.)

Here is a simple procedure to follow to make your book after you've written your story and made preliminary drafts of the illustrations and the text layouts.

- **Divide the story into sections.**
- **Make a guide sheet.**
- **Use the guide to lay out your pages.**
- **Review the parts of a book.**
- **Design the pages.**
- **Print more copies (optional).**
- **Bind the book.**
- **Decorate the cover.**
- **Make a bookplate and a bookmark.**

Now that you have an overview of the process, you are ready to begin.

Divide the Story into Sections

Decide what will be on each page—the writing and the illustrations. Look at the fairy tale on the following pages written by Mr. Bombino's class in Outlook, Washington. The layout may give you some ideas for dividing your own story.

The Dragon and the Mask Maker

Once upon a time in a distant land, there was a poor mask maker who lived in a stone cottage not far from a castle. 1.

In his cottage there were masks — masks hanging from the ceiling and unfinished masks on his work table. 2.

One day he loaded his cart with masks and headed toward the castle to try and sell some masks to the king and queen. 3.

He hadn't gone far before one of the wheels fell off his cart and he said, "Oh, fudge." 4.

After he had fixed his cart, he continued toward the castle. 5.

When the mask maker reached the castle, he went to the king and queen and said, "Would you like to buy some masks?" 6.

The king said, "We don't want your masks because of the legends we've heard about them." 7.

The mask maker said, "These masks aren't evil!" But the king said, "Please leave." 8.

So the mask maker left the castle and went back to the cottage.

9.

When he got home, he started to make masks of the exact likeness of the King and queen because he thought they might like them.

10.

The king mask had white hair and a white beard, and it had a beautiful crown on its head.

11.

The queen mask was beautiful with rosy cheeks, blue eyes, long brown hair and a lovely crown.

12.

Then he loaded his cart and headed back toward the castle.

13.

He didn't notice he was being followed by a dragon.

14.

The dragon was green and slimy with long, slender wings. He was breathing smoke from his nostrils and he was covered with scales with one golden scale on his forehead.

15.

The mask maker arrived at the castle and showed his new masks to the king and queen. He said, "I've come with masks I've made especially for you."

16.

The queen said, "They're beautiful."

But the king said, "Get out of here! They are bringing evil spirits." (He could see the dragon behind the mask maker.)

17. 18.

The mask maker was angry. He turned around to leave... and there was the dragon.

The mask maker had an idea. He put one of the masks on his face and the other one on the back of his head. Then he started walking toward the dragon—slowly, carefully—sideways, this way and that, until he was turning in circles heading toward the dragon.

19. 20.

The dragon thought the mask maker was an evil spirit. He started backing up and whining.

GULP

As the dragon backed across the drawbridge, he slipped and fell into the moat and he was eaten by the alligators.

21. 22.

The king said, "Thanks for killing the dragon. I want to buy all your masks for my soldiers to wear to scare off dragons."

The mask maker was hired and given a place to work in the palace as the royal mask maker for the king and queen, and he lived happily for the rest of his days.

23. 24.

Make a Guide Sheet

You will need a sheet of 8½"x11" white paper, a pencil or a fine line pen, and a ruler. Recreate this guide form.

1. Fold the sheet to find the center, and place a light dot at the top and the bottom.

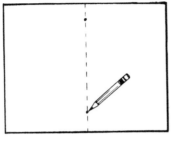

2. Measure ¼" to the left and ¼" to the right of these dots, and draw the two central guidelines.

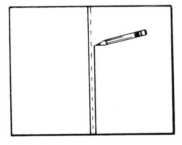

3. Measure ½" from the outside edge on both sides, and draw the two outside guidelines.

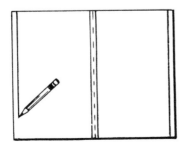

Your guide form is ready.

Use the Guide to Lay Out Your Pages

You will need blank sheets of paper and a pencil or a black, fine line pen to write the words and draw the illustrations on the paper. (You might want to draw the illustrations on individual sheets and glue them in place.)

To use the guide, place a blank sheet of white 8½"x11" paper on top of the guide form for each **two pages** that you make. (Since the pages are folded, you are actually making two pages at a time.) Before you begin, study the blank storyboard on the following page to get an idea of how your book will look. You might even want to make a quick-sketch storyboard for your own story before you begin writing it out and illustrating. Notice that you need some special pages at the front and the back of the book (front matter and back matter). Look over the definitions for these special pages so you can design your book just like a high-quality, hardbound book.

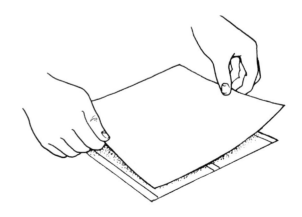

Blank Storyboard for a French-fold Book

(right side)   (left side)

Half-Title Page	Blank

Title Page	Copyright Page

Dedication Page	Blank

Foreword or Preface *(optional)*	Blank

Introduction *(optional)*	Blank

List of Illustrators *(for a group book)*	(continued)

First Page of Text	
1.	2.

3.	4.

5.	6.

7.	8.

9.	10.

11.	12.

13.	14.

15.	16.

17.	18.

Author Page	Colophon

Review the Parts of a Book

All the preliminary information about a book is called the **front matter**. These pages include the following:

- **Half-Title Page.** Only the title is written; no other information appears on this page.

- **Title Page.** This page shows the title, author, sometimes the illustrator, the publishing company and its location. (You need only the title, author, and location where the book was made.)

- **Copyright Page.** The copyright page is on the back of the title page. It contains the copyright notice which legally protects the text from being copied without permission of the copyright holder. The copyright notice has three parts: the copyright symbol (©), the year the book was published, and the name of the copyright holder. Also found on this page is the phrase "All rights reserved" and the publisher's address. Lots of other information can appear on this page, but this is all you really need. (If you want to be a good book detective, read the copyright pages of books to see how much you can learn about the publishing history of the books. You might even find a dedication on the copyright page if the publisher did not want to use an entire page for one.)

- **Dedication Page.** The dedication page is the next right-hand page across from the copyright page. You can dedicate your book to anyone that you

admire. It is a sign of honor or respect. Here are two sample dedications to give you some ideas:

For the great storytellers and bookmakers who have inspired this book

Dedicated with love to my parents

- **Foreword** (optional). Sometimes the author asks a friend or someone who is an authority about the author's subject to write something about the book he has just written. The person writing the foreword will point out the good things in the book. This will make the reader want to jump in and read the book.

- **Preface** (optional). Sometimes the author wants to say something to the reader about how he happened to write the book, or how he did research for the book. If he does, he puts it in the preface. The preface does not have to be signed by the author.

- **Introduction** (optional). If the author wants to tell the reader important information about how to use the book, he will put it in the introduction. The introduction will then be considered part of the text, and the page numbering will start here.

*Note: If this is a group book, you will want to include a **list of illustrators** with the page numbers and the names of the children who illustrated the pages.*

All the reference information about the book is called the **back matter**. These pages include the following:

- **Author Page.** Information about the author is often seen on the last page or inside back cover if the book doesn't have a separate dust jacket (the paper wrapping on hardbound books). Information about the illustrator may appear here, too. Sometimes a photograph is included.

- **Colophon.** The publisher, the printer, and the designer (that could be one person) may be so proud of the final result they will add a colophon to the last page to tell the reader how the book was made. They will say what kind of type was used for printing, what kind of paper they used, and how the book was bound. If the book is a limited edition, the copies might be numbered. Here are two examples:

Paper Masks and Puppets was set in Optima type and printed by Magna Color Press, Inc., Seattle, Washington. The pages were Smyth bound and glued to the cover by Bayless Bindery, Seattle, to make this a permanent book.

The Dragon and the Maskmaker was hand-printed and photocopied on a Minolta copy machine. The French-fold pages were bound with a heavy-duty stapler and cloth tape. The cover was decorated with original block prints carved from erasers.

Design the Pages

Now you are ready to design your pages. After you write in the necessary information on the pages that will be the front matter of your book, you are ready to write out the text and put in the final illustrations.

Place blank white paper (8½″ x 11″) over the guide form to help you decide how much space you have for the words and illustrations. Pay attention to the margins. Remember not to go outside the guidelines. You need the margin space for folding and binding the pages.

Review the storyboard (page 54), Mr. Bombino's class story, and the examples on page 46 for design ideas. Think about how you will place your text with your illustrations.

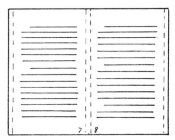
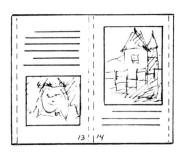

Print your words neatly, and make your drawings clear. Your final illustrations should be clean, dark line drawings made with a #2 pencil or a black, fine line pen if you are going to make several copies on a photocopy machine. Make bold lines like those found in a coloring book. Remember **not** to go outside the guidelines.

If you want to change something in your illustration, you might want to place a new paper over the illustration, put it up against a window, and trace over it. This can clean up your drawing and let you rearrange it, if necessary. When you finish the text and illustrations, write in any back matter you choose to include.

Note: If you are making a group book, give each child a section of the story to illustrate. That way every member of the group will have an illustration in the book. Illustrations can be glued in after the words have been written.

Remember to use a #2 pencil or a fine line pen so the pages can be printed on a copy machine. Don't color the illustrations—they can be colored after the pages have been printed.

Print More Copies (Optional)

After the pages have been completed, you will need to copy them if you want extra copies of your book to share with others. You can do this quickly and inexpensively on a photocopy machine. You will need one set of pages for each book you plan to bind.

Bind the Book

Fold the pages, and stack them in order by following these directions.

- Place each page face down and fold in half so the words and illustrations are on the outside.

- Stack the pages in order with the fold on the left. (When you reach the numbered text pages, the even numbers will show on top of the stack.)

- Turn the stack of folded pages over when you have finished folding, and check the order. (Hold the open edges in your left hand, and slowly let your fingers "walk" through the pages as you check them.)

- Set the pages aside.

Prepare the paper for the covers and the endpapers by following these steps.

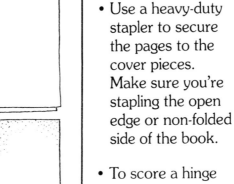

- Make the cover pieces. Cut front and back covers (5½"x8½") from any heavy board: poster board or railroad board work well.

- Make the endpapers. Cut four endpapers (5½"x8½") from construction paper.

Now you're ready to assemble your book.

- Glue one endpaper to the inside of each cover piece. Place the remaining two endpapers on either side of the book pages.

- Insert the folded pages and endpapers between the cover pieces.

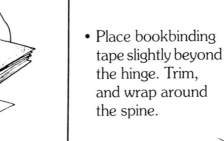

- Use a heavy-duty stapler to secure the pages to the cover pieces. Make sure you're stapling the open edge or non-folded side of the book.

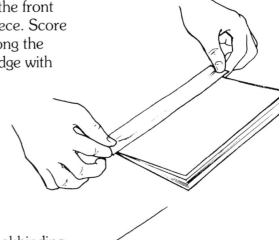

- To score a hinge so the cover will open easily, place a ruler about ½" from the outside edge of the front cover piece. Score a line along the ruler's edge with scissors.

- Place bookbinding tape slightly beyond the hinge. Trim, and wrap around the spine.

Materials for Decorating the Cover, Bookplate, and Bookmark

Erasers (The eraser prints used in this book were made from Staedtler giant drafting erasers—1½"x3"x½".)
Pencil
Ruler
Scrap paper
Stamp pad
Speedball linoleum cutters: Linozip set
Glue stick or Elmer's Glue-All
Construction paper:
    for cover decoration, 4½"x8"
    for background piece, 4⅝"x8¼"
    for title piece, 3½"x2¼"
    for background piece, 3⅝"x2⅜"
    for bookplate, 2½"x3½"
    for bookmark, 1½"x10"

Optional:
Compass
Black, fine line pen

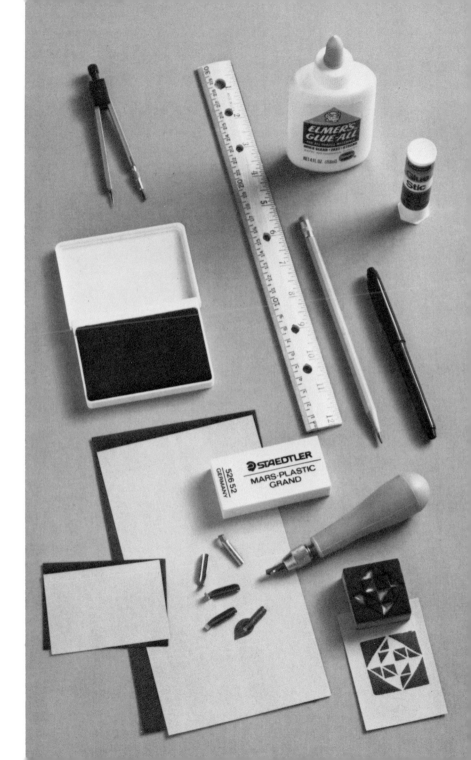

Decorate the Cover

Now that your book is bound, you are ready to decorate the cover. There are many ways to decorate. One way is to create interesting patterns with carved erasers. All you need are a few simple tools and an eraser to make a stamp. You can use any eraser and cut it into any size you like. (If you cut a giant Staedtler eraser in half, you will have two squares, 1½"x1½".) There are two ways to put a design on your eraser before carving.

1. Draw a design on the eraser with a pencil. (A compass and ruler may be used, if desired.)

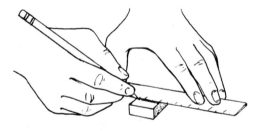

2. Draw a design on paper, place the eraser on the design, and press firmly to transfer the design to the eraser. You can practice making designs until you come up with the one you want to transfer to the eraser. Trace around the eraser to make several work spaces. Then draw in your designs. Choose the design you like best to transfer to the eraser.

When your design is on the eraser, cut away areas with Speedball linoleum cutters. The design will change depending on what sections of the eraser you remove. Look at the following examples for ideas.

resulting print

Draw the cutting blade toward you along the line. You will cut intersecting, indented lines into the eraser. The four triangle spaces will be raised.

resulting print

To emphasize a negative space, cut away a larger area.

After your stamp is finished, cut a piece of construction paper 4½"x8". Stamp the construction paper for the cover decoration. (Be sure to put scrap paper underneath in case the pattern you are stamping goes off the edge of the decoration piece.)

scrap paper

Glue the decorated paper to the front cover. (You might want to add a background piece.) The title of the book can be written on a smaller sheet of paper, glued to a background piece, and attached to the decorated cover.

Here are a few examples of decorated covers to give you some ideas.

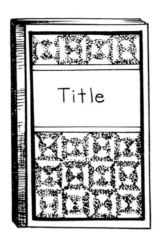

Make a Bookplate and a Bookmark

After your book is finished, you'll want to add some finishing touches. You can make a bookplate and a bookmark by cutting some extra construction paper and printing it with the same design you used to decorate your book cover. Here are some examples:

This book belongs to:

This book belongs to:

Glue the bookplate to the inside of the front cover.

Use your bookmark when desired.

Read your book and enjoy!

So . . .

Keep making masks,
writing fairy tales, and
making books . . .

and may you live happily ever after.

Bibliography

Fairy Tale References for Kids

Andersen, Hans Christian. *The Complete Fairy Tales & Stories*. Translated from the Danish by Erik Christian Haugaard. Illustrated by Michael Foreman. New York: Doubleday, 1974.

Cauley, Lorinda Bryan. *Jack & the Beanstalk*. Retold & illustrated by Lorinda Bryan Cauley. New York: Putnam Publishing Group, 1983.

Ehrlich, Amy, adapted by. *The Random House Book of Fairy Tales*. Illustrated by Diane Goode. New York: Random, 1985.

The Fairy Tales of the Brothers Grimm. Fairy Tale Series. Illustrated by Arthur Rackham. New York: Abaris Books, 1984.

The Green Fairy Book. Collected by Andrew Lang. Edited by Brian Alderson. Illustrated by Anthony Maitland. Rev. ed. New York: Viking, 1978.

Grimm, Jacob, & Wilhelm K. Grimm. *Hansel & Gretel*. Illustrated by Susan Jeffers. New York: Dial Books for Young Readers, 1980.

_____. *Little Red Riding Hood*. Retold & illustrated by Trina Schart Hyman. New York: Holiday, 1982.

_____. *Snow-White & the Seven Dwarfs: A Tale from the Brothers Grimm*. Translated from the German by Randall Jarrell. Illustrated by Nancy Ekholm Burkert. New York: Farrar, Straus & Giroux, 1972.

Haviland, Virginia. *Favorite Fairy Tales Told in Norway*. Retold from Norse folklore by Virginia Haviland. Illustrated by Leonard Weisgard. Boston: Little, 1961. Stories adapted from the 1859 translation by Sir George Webb Dasent of Norwegian folktales gathered by Peter Christian Asbjornsen and Jorgen E. Moe.

Jacobs, Joseph, ed. *English Fairy Tales*. 3d ed. Collected by Joseph Jacobs. Illustrated by John D. Batten. 1898. Reprint. New York: Dover, 1967.

Mayer, Marianna. *Beauty & the Beast*. Illustrated by Mercer Mayer. New York: Macmillan, 1978.

Perrault, Charles. *Cinderella; or, The Little Glass Slipper*. Translated & illustrated by Marcia Brown. New York: Scribner, 1954.

_____. *Perrault's Complete Fairy Tales*. Translated from the French by A. E. Johnson & others. Illustrated by W. Heath Robinson. New York: Dodd, 1982.

Price, Margaret Evans. *Once Upon a Time: A Book of Old-Time Fairy Tales*. Illustrated by Margaret Evans Price. New York: Macmillan, 1986.

Yolen, Jane. *The Sleeping Beauty*. Retold by Jane Yolen. Illustrated by Ruth Sanderson. New York: Knopf, 1986.

Zelinsky, Paul O. *Rumpelstiltskin*. From the German of the Brothers Grimm. Retold & illustrated by Paul O. Zelinsky. New York: Dutton, 1986.

Further Reading for Adults

Andersen, Hans Christian. *The Complete Fairy Tales & Stories*. Translated by Erik Christian Haugaard. New York: Doubleday, n.d.

Bettelheim, Bruno. *The Uses of Enchantment: The Meaning & Importance of Fairy Tales*. New York: Knopf, 1976.

Brenner, Fred. "Designing and Illustrating Children's Picture Books." *The Artist's Magazine* 3 (May 1986): 68-98.

Carpenter, Humphrey, and Mari Prichard. *The Oxford Companion to Children's Literature*. New York: Oxford University Press, 1984.

Meyer, Susan E. *A Treasury of the Great Children's Book Illustrators*. New York: Abrams, 1983.

Opie, Iona, and Peter Opie. *The Classic Fairy Tales*. New York: Oxford University Press, 1974.

Sale, Roger. *Fairy Tales & After: From Snow White to E. B. White*. Cambridge: Harvard University Press, 1978.

Wilson, Adrian. *The Design of Books*. Layton, Utah: Gibbs M. Smith, 1974.

Yolen, Jane. *Touch Magic: Fantasy, Faerie & Folklore in Literature of Childhood*. New York: Putnam Publishing Group, Philomel, 1981.

About the Authors

Ron and Marsha Feller are professional storytellers. They have traveled throughout the United States and Canada telling stories, singing songs, and teaching boys and girls and adults how to make masks, write their own stories and songs, and make books. They are popular speakers at Young Writers' Conferences and educational seminars.

The Fellers live on the property of Morning Star Boys' Ranch in Spokane, Washington, where they have performed with the boys during the Christmas season for the past 22 years.

Ron and Marsha are the authors of *Paper Masks and Puppets for Stories, Songs and Plays.*

The Fellers can provide concerts and workshops as well as supplies for masks and books. For information write to:

The Arts Factory
P.O. Box 55547
Seattle, WA 98155

Fanciful Faces & Handbound Books: Fairy Tales was set in Souvenir type and printed by K&H Printers-Lithographers Inc., Everett, Washington. The pages were Smyth sewn and glued to the cover by Bayless Bindery, Seattle, to make this a permanent book.

808
Fel   Feller, Ron
       Fairy tales.

L